<u>INDEX</u>

Mossad Covert War

Mossad: Back in 2007

In an August 17 (2007) meeting, Israeli Mossad Chief Meir Dagan thanked Under Secretary Burns for America's support of Israel as evidenced by the previous day's signing of an MOU that provides Israel with USD 30 billion in security assistance from 2008-2018.

Dagan reviewed Israel's five-pillar strategy concerning Iran's nuclear program, stressed that Iran is economically vulnerable, and pressed for more activity with Iran's minority groups aimed at regime change.

Assessing the region, Dagan said Israel sees itself in the middle of a rapidly changing environment, in which the fate of one Middle Eastern country is connected to another. Turning to Iran, Dagan observed that it is in a transition period. Instability in Iran is driven by inflation and tension among ethnic minorities.

Dagan said that the Gulf states and Saudi Arabia are concerned about the growing importance of Iran and its influence on them. They are taking precautions, trying to increase their own military defensive capabilities. Referring to the Gulf Security Dialogue (GSD), Dagan warned that these countries would not be able to cope with the amount of weapons systems they intend to acquire: "They do not use the weapons effectively."

Turning to the Gulf Security Dialogue (GSD), Dagan said that enhancing the capabilities of the Gulf states "is the right direction to go," especially as they are afraid of Iran. Such a U.S. commitment will be a stabilizing factor in the region. Dagan clarified that he would not oppose U.S. security assistance to America's Arab partners. He expressed concern, nevertheless, about the current policies of those partners — especially with regards to Syria and Iran. Dagan added that if those countries must choose between buying defensive systems from the U.S. or France, then he would prefer they buy systems from the U.S., as this would bring them closer to the U.S.

Five Pillar Strategy

Dagan led discussion on Iran by pointing out that the U.S. and Israel have different timetables concerning when Iran is likely to acquire a nuclear capability. He clarified that the Israel Atomic Energy Commission's (IAEC) timetable is purely technical in nature, while the Mossad considers other factors, including the regime's determination to succeed. While Dagan acknowledged that there is still time to "resolve" the Iran nuclear crisis, he stressed that Iran is making a great effort to achieve a nuclear capability: "The threat is obvious, even if we have a different timetable. If we want to postpone their acquisition of a nuclear capability, then we have to invest time and effort ourselves."

Dagan described how the Israeli strategy consists of five pillars:

A) **Political Approach**: Dagan praised efforts to bring Iran before the UNSC, and signaled his agreement with the pursuit of a third sanctions resolution. He acknowledged that pressure on Iran is building up, but said this approach alone will not resolve the crisis. He stressed that the timetable for political action is different than the nuclear project's timetable.

B) **Covert Measures**: Dagan and the Under Secretary agreed not to discuss this approach in the larger group setting.

C) **Counter-proliferation**: Dagan underscored the need to prevent know-how and technology from making their way to Iran, and said that more can be done in this area.

D) **Sanctions**: Dagan said that the biggest successes had so far been in this area. Three Iranian banks are on the verge of collapse. The financial sanctions are having a nationwide impact. Iran's regime can no longer just deal with the bankers themselves.

E) **Force Regime Change**: Dagan said that more should be done to foment regime change in Iran, possibly with the support of student democracy movements, and ethnic groups (e.g., Azeris, Kurds, Baluchs) opposed to the ruling regime.

Dagan clarified that the U.S., Israel and like-minded countries must push on all five pillars at the same time. Some are bearing fruit now; others would bear fruit in due time, especially if more attention were placed on them. Dagan urged more attention on regime change, asserting that more could be done to develop the identities of ethnic minorities in Iran. He said he was sure that Israel and the U.S. could "change the ruling regime in Iran, and its attitude towards backing terror regimes." He added, "We could also get them to delay their nuclear project. Iran could become a normal state."

Dagan stressed that Iran has weak spots that can be exploited. According to his information, unemployment exceeds 30 percent nationwide, with some towns and villages experiencing 50 percent unemployment, especially among 17-30 year olds. Inflation averages more than 40 percent, and people are criticizing the government for investing in and sponsoring Hamas, saying that they government should invest in Iran itself. "The economy is hurting," he said, "and this is provoking a real crisis among Iran's leaders." He added that Iran's minorities are "raising their heads, and are tempted to resort to violence."

Dagan suggested that more could be done to get the Europeans to take a tougher stand against Iran. Under Secretary Burns agreed, and suggested that Israel could help by reaching out to the Europeans. Dagan said that Israel is already doing this, and would continue to do so. Dagan reiterated the need to strike at Iran's heart by engaging with its people directly.

Voice of America (VOA) broadcasts are important, but more radio transmissions in Farsi are needed. Coordination with the Gulf states is helpful, but the U.S. should also coordinate with Azerbaijan and countries to the north of Iran, to put pressure on Iran. Russia, he said, would be annoyed, but it would be fitting, as Russia appears bent on showing the U.S. that it cannot act globally without considering Russia.

Under Secretary Burns stressed that the USG is focused on Iran not only because of its nuclear program, but also because it supports terrorism and Shiite militias in Iraq. The U.S. approach is currently focused on the diplomatic track and increasing pressure on Iran through sanctions. Work in the UNSC helps to define the Iranian nuclear threat as one that affects international security, and not just that of Israel.

While UNSC members Russia, China and Qatar will water down efforts to increase pressure on Iran, it is still worthwhile to push for a third sanctions resolution. In the meantime, the U.S. will encourage the Europeans, Japan and South Korea to implement unilateral sanctions against Iran outside the UNSC framework. The U.S. will continue to encourage banks and financial institutions to slow down their operations in Iran and financially isolate it.

Regarding military pressure, the Under Secretary noted that the U.S. has deployed 1-2 carrier battle groups in the Gulf over the last six months, and that President Bush has stated that he will interrupt Iran's activity in Iraq. As for outreach to the Iranian people, the VOA is now broadcasting programs in Farsi, and the USG is trying to get more Iranian students to visit the U.S. to promote people-to-people relations.

Iran's counter intelligence

In its ongoing shadow war with Israel, the Iranian side's lone "success" was the July 18 bombing of a Bulgarian bus carrying Israeli tourists — though European investigators last week officially attributed that attack to Iran's Lebanese proxy, Hizballah. That leaves the Islamic Republic itself with a failure rate hovering near 100% abroad and an operational tempo — nine overseas plots uncovered in nine months — that carries a whiff of desperation. A Tehran government long branded by U.S. officials as the globe's leading exporter of terrorism may be cornering the market on haplessness.

Within Iran's own borders, however, the story is different. Twice in the past two years Iranian intelligence has cracked espionage rings working with Israel's Mossad. In both cases, the arrests were the furthest thing from secret: announced at a news conference, each was later followed up by televised confessions broadcast on Iranian state television in prime time. Given Iran's history of trumped-up confessions, skepticism is more than justified. But the arrests appear to be solid. One intelligence official said the captured Iranians provided "support and logistics" to the Mossad operatives who carried out the assassinations of Iranian nuclear scientists.

At least four scientists were killed on Tehran's streets from 2010 to 2012, when Israel ratcheted back on covert operations inside Iran. Officially, Israel has remained silent on the killings, though government officials will coyly say they welcome the deaths. The Jewish state maintains the same ambiguous posture on other "setbacks" to Iran's nuclear program widely — and correctly, Western intelligence officials say — attributed to Mossad, from the Stuxnet computer virus, to mysterious explosions like the massive blast at a missile base, which destroyed ballistic missiles that could reach Israel.

The covert onslaught dovetails with Israel's history of reaching "over the horizon" to disarm perceived threats at a distance. To keep advanced arms from reaching Hamas and Hizballah, Israel in the past year sent warplanes to bomb convoys and arms depots in Sudan and Syria, respectively, without apparent retribution. In the case of Iran, however, experts say the audacity of Israel's covert campaign stirred Tehran to revive an espionage effort that lay largely fallow since 9/11. The *Spy vs. Spy* contest that ensued would prove woefully one-sided, even in the third-world countries where Iran chose to strike, hoping to avoid heightened security awareness in the developed world. In the end, its only success came inside Iran, where the secret police operate without inhibition.

Mossad 's killings

The shadow war may have started on Jan. 15, 2007, the day Ardeshir Hosseinpour passed away. Hosseinpour was a specialist in electromagnetics at the Nuclear Technology Center in the city of Isfahan, Iran, but his death might have escaped notice had Iran's government not kept it under wraps for almost a week, finally attributing it to fumes from a faulty heater. An online report by the American private intelligence firm Stratfor suggested another cause — radioactive poisoning — and hinted that Mossad's Caesarea section was back in business.

Caesarea, named for an Israeli beach town that dates back to Roman times, is the operations branch of Israel's secret service, most notoriously responsible for the assassinations of some two dozen Palestinians (and an innocent waiter) after the 1972 Munich Olympics. Assassinations are carried out by a very small unit dubbed Kidon, the Hebrew word for "tip of the spear." Kidon operates at a remove from the legions of Mossad employees working in less lethal fields.

It would have been a unit called Hatzomet, or "The Junction," that recruited Majid Fashi, a handsome young Iranian who dropped out of high school to pursue a career in kickboxing. By the account he gave on Iranian state television early in 2011, Fashi presented himself at the Israeli consulate in Istanbul in 2007 and was vetted for a solid year before being shown any trust. Two years later, on Jan. 12, 2010, he would place a bomb on a motorbike parked on the sidewalk outside the Tehran home of Masoud Ali Mohammadi; the nuclear physicist was killed when it was detonated by remote control.

In the broadcast, Fashi accurately described the Mossad campus north of Tel Aviv. He said he had been given a laptop equipped with a second operating system and used it to communicate through online drop boxes. He was impressed by his handlers' thoroughness. At one point Fashi described studying a scale model of Ali Mohammadi's street. "It was an exact copy of the real one," Fashi said. "The tree next it, the street curb, the bridge." In a later broadcast, he was seated across from Ali Mohammadi's widow, who glared at him as he bowed his head and wept. Mossad officials were "pissed off and shocked" seeing their agent on television, the intelligence official said.

Fashi was executed in May 2012. About the same time, Iran's intelligence minister announced the arrest of 14 more Iranians, eight men and six women dubbed members of the "Terror Club" in the subsequent prime-time broadcast of that name. Filmed in shadow, and rich in atmospherics, the Aug. 5 program recreated Ali mohammadi's death and four subsequent attacks: they started with the Nov. 29, 2010 nearly simultaneous attempts on Majid Shariari and Fereydoun Abbasi, nuclear scientists driving to work when magnetic "sticky bombs" were attached to the side of their cars from passing motorcycles. Abbasi managed to escape before it detonated, saving his wife as well. Shariari was killed — a significant setback for the Iranian nuclear program where he was the top scientist, according to a Western intelligence official.

The confessed agents offered absorbing detail — they were aboard a Bajaj Pulsar, wearing helmets, when the magnet bomb stuck on the right front panel of Shariari's car exploded. The riders scrambled into the "trail car" assigned to follow the target and disappeared into the traffic of the Imam Ali Autobahn. Already gone was the car assigned to cut off and slow the car carrying the scientist. They claimed to have rehearsed on a practice track inside Israel. None of the details could be confirmed, but an intelligence official acknowledged: "Another network was taken."

The third scientist, Dariush Rezaeinejad was shot on July 23, 2011 after picking up his child at a day care; his wife described hearing shots whiz by as she chased the assailants. The most recent assassination was the Jan. 11, 2012 death of Mustafa Ahmadi-Roshan, an expert on uranium enrichment, also by a magnet bomb slapped on his car during his morning commute.

By then, Iran was trying to strike back. The task of avenging the scientists fell to the sprawling Quds Force's own covert-operations division, known as Unit 400. It took a shotgun approach, targeting Israeli diplomatic missions in a variety of countries, mostly in the developing world where the global antiterrorism mesh is not so fine. Exposed in Baku, Tbilisi, Johannesburg, Mombasa and Bangkok, the failures mounted at a pace that was itself one of the problems.

In the world of espionage, a quality covert operation can take years to pull together. Yet in the 15 months from May 2011 to July 2012, the Quds Force and Hizballah attempted 20 attacks, by the count of Matthew Levitt, a former State Department counterterrorism official. "Hizballah and the Quds Force traded speed for tradecraft and reaped what they sowed," Levitt writes in a January report for the Washington Institute for Near East Policy. "Quds Force planners were stretched thin by the rapid tempo of their new attack plan, and were forced to throw together random teams of operatives who had not trained together."

The decline in quality was so striking it initially inspired disbelief. Recall the preposterous-sounding plot weaving together a former used-car salesman, Mexico's Zetas drug gang and a bank transfer from a Revolutionary Guard account to assassinate Saudi Arabia's ambassador — by bombing a Washington restaurant? A year on it looks like the new normal.

In Bangkok, an Iranian agent entered a courtroom in a wheelchair, having accidentally blown his legs off while fleeing police. A January alert issued by Turkish intelligence was light on specifics but quite certain the Quds operatives would be staying in five-star hotels.

"There's a number of reasons that Iranian intelligence has suffered," says Meir Javedanfar, an Iranian-born analyst who lectures at the Interdisciplinary Center in Herzliya, Israel. "No. 1," he says, "is the 2009 uprisings in Iran." The street protests over a fraudulent election undermined the perceived legitimacy of the state among people who once would work for it, including in its secret services. "People less and less see it as a nationalist endeavor and more as a Khamenei-related project to strengthen himself," Javedanfar says, referring to Iran's Supreme Leader Ayatullah Ali Khamenei, who by some published accounts personally authorizes all overseas attacks.

Hard-liners further aggravated the situation by purging competent reformists from both the secret services and from Iran's embassies — crucial to a force expected to work undetected abroad. "Basically the Quds Force doesn't cooperate with the Foreign Ministry, and the Foreign Ministry isn't what it used to be either," says Javedanfar. Under President Mahmoud Ahmadinejad, 42% of ministry employees have only high school degrees. "The regime is a bigger threat to itself than Israel," he says.

Reva Bhalla, a senior analyst with Stratfor, the US private intelligence company with strong government security connections, said the strategy was to take out key people. "With co-operation from the United States, Israeli covert operations have focused both on eliminating key human assets involved in the nuclear programme and in sabotaging the Iranian nuclear supply chain," she said. "As US-Israeli relations are bound to come under strain over the Obama administration's outreach to Iran, and as the political atmosphere grows in complexity, an intensification of Israeli covert activity against Iran is likely to result."

"Israel has shown no hesitation in assassinating weapons scientists for hostile regimes in the past," said a European intelligence official, speaking on condition of anonymity. They did it with Iraq and they will do it with Iran when they can."

Mossad's covert operations cover a range of activities. Israeli and US intelligence co-operated with European companies working in Iran to obtain photographs and other confidential material about Iranian nuclear and missile sites. Israel has also used front companies to infiltrate the Iranian purchasing network that the clerical regime uses to circumvent United Nations sanctions and obtain so-called "dual use" items — metals, valves, electronics, machinery – for its nuclear programme.

The businesses initially supply Iran with legitimate material, winning Tehran's trust, and then start to deliver faulty or defective items that "poison" the country's atomic activities. "Without military strikes, there is still considerable scope for disrupting and damaging the Iranian programme and this has been done with some success," said Yossi Melman, a prominent Israeli journalist who covers security and intelligence issues for the Haaretz newspaper.

Mossad and Western intelligence operations have also infiltrated the Iranian nuclear programme and "bought" information from prominent atomic scientists. Israel has later selectively leaked some details to its allies, the media and United Nations atomic agency inspectors.

But Vince Canastraro, the former CIA counter-terrorism chief, expressed doubts about the efficacy of secret Israeli operations against Iran. "You cannot carry out foreign policy objectives via covert operations," he said. "You can't get rid of a couple of people and hope to affect Iran's nuclear capability."

The future of covert operations

A Time Magazine report revealed that Israeli intelligence services have scaled back their covert operations inside Iran. According to senior security officials who spoke to the magazine, operations have been reduced in areas such as high-profile missions, including assassinations and detonations at Iranian missile bases, as well as in recruiting spies inside the Iranian nuclear program, and efforts to gather on-the-ground intelligence.

The report further states that according to one official, the reductions have caused "increasing dissatisfaction" inside the Mossad, Israel's intelligence agency. Another official credits the reduced activities to the reluctance of Prime Minister Benjamin Netanyahu, who the official says is worried about the outcome of the operations being discovered.

Scaling back covert operations against Iran carries costs especially as Iran hurries to disperse its centrifuges into facilities deep underground. In one intelligence finding, an Israeli official says Iran itself estimates that sabotage to date has set back its centrifuge program by two full years. The computer virus known as Stuxnet is only the best known of a series of efforts to slow the Iranian program.

That effort involves a variety of governments besides Israel, involving equipment made to purposely malfunction after being tampered with before it physically entered Iran, says the report. The setbacks have prompted Iran to announce it would manufacture all components of its nuclear program itself – something outside experts are highly skeptical Tehran has the ability to actually do.

CIA Covert War

During both the Bush and Obama administrations, Iran and the United States have engaged in a shadow war that relies more on technology and human intelligence than conventional weaponry. Their covert campaigns include cyber attacks, espionage, and high-tech sabotage. Their common goal is to signal their resolve, impact each other's capabilities, and demonstrate the credibility of their deterrence – in turn swaying each other's decision-making.

The United States and Israel have reportedly worked together on a series of cyber attacks to slow or disrupt Iran's nuclear program since at least 2008. Although their origins are officially unknown, the Stuxnet worm reportedly attacked centrifuge production in late 2009 or early 2010, while the Flame virus collected information on Iranian officials in 2012.

The United States and Iran have used drones to gather intelligence and signal their offensive, defensive, and deterrent capabilities against each other. Drone technology has been an increasingly integral part of the United States intelligence and military arsenal over the past two decades. U.S. drones are far more advanced; they have been reportedly deployed in Afghanistan, Iraq, Libya, Pakistan and Yemen.

U.S. drone operations over Iran began after the start of the Afghanistan war; they reportedly increased after the 2003 invasion of Iraq. Specifics are classified but drones almost certainly monitored anti-American insurgent activity organized on Iranian territory. Over the last few years, drones may have spied on a wider array of Tehran's assets, including its nuclear program.

Iran's drone technology has also improved in recent years, possibly with help from Russia and China. Tehran unveiled the Karrar —its first home-made long-range drone—in August 2010. But experts have been skeptical about its capabilities and Iran's ability to guide the drone over long distances. In September 2012, the Revolutionary Guards unveiled the Shahed 129, an attack and surveillance drone with a purported range of up to 1,200 miles.

Tehran reportedly captured a U.S. RQ-170 Sentinel drone in late 2011 and subsequently claimed to have decoded its data and copied its technology. In late 2012, Iran claimed that it captured a U.S. ScanEagle drone, which the United States denied. But in December 2012, Secretary of Defense Leon E. Panetta warned that the United States needs to keep track of the surveillance capability of Iran's drones.

Like many military platforms, drones can accomplish a variety of objectives. In October 2012, Israel shot down an Iranian drone reportedly near Dimona, where Israel's nuclear weapons program is believed to be based. The drone was reportedly launched by the Lebanese militia Hezbollah, which is supplied by Iran. The use of this drone may have been intended to gather intelligence and test Israeli defensive capabilities, but also to signal the potential for an Iranian strike on Dimona in retaliation for a future U.S. or Israeli attack on

Iran.

Military activities always entail the risk of an unintentional escalation. Iranian fighter jets reportedly fired on a U.S. drone over the Persian Gulf on November 1, but they failed to hit it. While no escalation developed in this case, the increasing build-up of opposing forces in the Gulf has raised the risk of an entanglement. Escalation would be even more likely to occur if one side attacks a military objective in international waters.

Iran is a powerful regional player, but it is not a superpower with the global ambitions of the former Soviet Union. Iran's gross domestic product pales in comparison to some individual U.S. states. It has limited ability to project beyond its borders, other than through proxies such as Hezbollah and Hamas.

Tehran wants to impose costs on the United States and Israel for their covert programs and to block or dissuade their further moves against the Islamic Republic. Iran's actions also demonstrate its ability to fight back unconventionally tit-for-tat. Iran is also signaling to key players in the Gulf, notably Saudi Arabia and the United Arab Emirates, that their help in any attack on Iran could carry hidden or unanticipated costs. Iran's actions are also probably driven by domestic politics. The government would have risked a loss of credibility if it had not responded to cyber attacks and assassinations of scientists.

Covert campaigns are integral to both U.S. and Iranian efforts. But they almost certainly cannot achieve the long-term objectives of either country. U.S. covert action is unlikely to compel Iran to fulfill its international obligations on its nuclear program. Iranian covert action is also unlikely to undermine U.S. resolve either

Mossad – Saudi Intel Partnership

Stratfor leaks

While publicly underplaying the significance of WikiLeaks activity in combating government secrecy, senior execs and analysts at private US intelligence firm Stratfor privately described WikiLeaks founder Julian Assange as a "terrorist" and "delusion nut" who "needs to be water-boarded" and made to "move from country to country" for the "next 25 years". The emails, part of over five million ones to be released, also suggest that senior Stratfor staff were apparently aware of secret charges reportedly by the US government to indict Assange and didn't mind using "trumped up" charges to lock up the whistle blower well before WikiLeaks had gone after Stratfor.

Most of the Stratfor email exchanges dealing with WikiLeaks and Assange are between mid-2010 to mid-2011. By 2010, WikiLeaks had already made a name for itself. It had published a number of ground-breaking documents dealing with a wide range of topics, including secret Guantanamo Bay procedures, the Climategate emails, the 2008 Peru oil scandal, the Milton report on toxic dumping in Africa, thousands of pager messages made during 9/11 and more. Despite all this, 2010 would be the year that truly elevated the organization, with release of the infamous "Collateral Murder" video, the Afghan War Diary, the Iraq War logs, and more than 250,000 US diplomatic cables.

According to the emails, Stratfor began to turn its eye to WikiLeaks in 2010, particularly in regards to the releases pertaining to the United States. Stratfor was well aware of the Cablegate scandal months before WikiLeaks officially announced the release in 22 November 2010. In an email dated 6 June 2010, Fred Burton, Stratfor's vice-president for counter-terrorism and corporate security and former special agent with the US Diplomatic Security Service, converses with Michael Psillico, a US state department official, over the arrest of Bradley Manning for his alleged role in providing material to WikiLeaks.

The emails, dated 2 May 2007, show discussions between Fred Burton, Stratfor's vice-president of counter-terrorism, and analysts in regards to the alleged secret Saudi-Israeli intelligence alliance. The email exchange also shows that Stratfor execs considered pursuing their own business relationship with the Saudi monarchy or, as Burton called them, "sleezy arsehole ragheads."

Cyprus

Burton forwarded a short message to the general analyst email list which recounted HUMINT (human intelligence) on the alleged secret deal. The source claimed that Mossad offered covert assistance to the Saudis with "intelligence collection and advice on Iran." The city of Nicosia in Cyprus was cited in the email "as a primary transit hub into Riyadh."

Additionally, the source advised Burton that the Saudis "are playing both sides of the fence – with the jihadists and the Israelis – for fear that the US does not have a handle on either." The source also claimed that "several enterprising Mossad officers, both past and present, are making a bundle selling the Saudis everything from security equipment, intelligence and consultation," a statement that implies an established security and business relationship between the Jewish state and the Saudi monarchy.

The message by Burton was additionally shared with another list that included Stratfor's president and Chief Financial Officer Don Kuykendall. Burton inquired, "Have we got the Saudi Foreign Ministry or intel[ligence] services as sub clients? If not, [I] suggest we send Mike Parks [Stratfor employee with a history of getting clients for Stratfor], who is good friends with Prince Bandar, to sign them up. $100,000 deal is nothing to these folks. I think Les Janka also has contacts with these sleezy arsehole ragheads (sic)."

The idea seemed to resonate well with other Stratfor senior staff, although there were concerns whether Stratfor's budget would cover an employee's trip to Riyadh in order to charm out a deal. The email thread ended with Burton, typically tasteless in his humor, asking, "Either we want these towel heads as a client o[r] not. I can also have anybody we send to Riyadh beheaded."

The year 2007 was the year when Saudi Arabia officially reaffirmed its support for the Arab Peace Initiative. Moreover, a New York Times report in August of that year stated that Saudi Arabia's foreign minister, Prince Saud al-Faisal, was keen to be involved in the ill-fated Annapolis peace conference due to occur in the fall. In turn, Israel signaled its 'openness' to the Saudi plan.

Stuxnet malware

Saudi Arabia and Israel's Mossad intelligence division are co-conspiring to produce a computer worm "more destructive" than the Stuxnet malware to sabotage Iran's nuclear program. Ex- Saudi spy chief Prince Bandar bin Sultan and director of Israel's Mossad intelligence agency Tamir Bardo sent their representatives to a meeting in Vienna on November 24, 2013 to increase the two sides' cooperation in intelligence and sabotage operations against Iran's nuclear program. One of the major methods discussed was "the production of a malware worse than...Stuxnet."

Stuxnet, a computer worm discovered in 2010, formed the basis of a cyberattack that sabotaged Iran's uranium enrichment program. Its complexity prompted researchers to claim that it could only have been developed by a nation state. It was generally believed to have been developed by the US and Israel, with former NSA contractor and whistleblower Edward Snowden only confirming their covert roles in an interview in July 2013.

The intention behind the development of the new malware would be to spy on and destroy the software structure of Iran's nuclear program. The two spy chiefs brought with them teams of Israeli and Saudi cyber specialists to discuss "the production of a malware worse than Stuxnet to spy on and destroy the software structure of Iran's nuclear program. The plan would need a great deal of time and funding, with a rough figure of US $1 million being given as an estimate. It was apparently welcomed by Saudi Arabia with open arms.

New meeting

Saudi ex-spy chief Bandar met with Mossad's Bardo in Jordan's Aqaba port city, inciting some concern from Saudi Arabia's Crown Prince Salman bin Abdulazi, who had advised against Bandar engaging in direct consultations, instead deeming 'clandestine' discussions with Israel over strategic Middle Eastern issues more appropriate.

A recent agreement between Iran and the Group 5+1 (the US, Russia, China, France and Britain plus Germany) unsettled Saudi officials, with Bandar having previously denounced the interim deal as the *"West's treachery."* Israeli Prime Minister Benjamin Netanyahu lambasted the agreement, which was reached on November 23, 2013 as *"a historic mistake."*

On November 17, 2013 *The Sunday Times* reported that the Israeli Mossad intelligence agency and Saudi officials were working together to develop a contingency plan should Iran's nuclear program not be adequately curtailed. Both governments reportedly expressed concern that negotiations could result in concessions being made to Iran.

Meeting in Tel Aviv

CIA chief John Brennan made a "secret" visit to Israel to discuss an emerging nuclear deal between Iran and world powers, Israel's leftist *Haaretz* newspaper reported.
The visit came as a June 30, 2015 deadline looms for a deal that would row back Iran's nuclear program in return for relief from sanctions, which Israel has long opposed, causing friction between Jerusalem and the White House.

Brennan met his counterpart, Mossad chief Tamir Pardo, and other intelligence officials, as well as Prime Minister Binyamin Netanyahu, *Haaretz* reported, citing "senior Israeli officials." They discussed the emerging Iran deal and Tehran's "subversive" activities around the Middle East.

The report surfaces after Brennan stressed on *CBS News* last week that there is a "very, very strong relationship between United States and Israel on the intelligence, security and military fronts."

"It's one of the great things, I think, about our system; there can be policy differences between our governments but the intelligence and security professionals know that we have an obligation to keep our countries safe and secure," he added.

"And so although there's been great debate about the Iranian nuclear negotiations that are ongoing," continued Brennan, "the CIA, NSA and other intelligence community entities are working very close with their Israeli as well as other counterparts."

GREAT MIDDLE EAST PROJECT

Longstanding neocon dreams to partition Iraq into three along ethnic and religious lines have been resurrected. White House officials now estimate that the fight against the region's 'Islamic State' will last years, and may outlive the Obama administration.

But this 'long war' vision goes back to nebulous ideas formally presented by late RAND Corp analyst Laurent Muraweic before the Pentagon's Defense Policy Board at the invitation of then chairman Richard Perle. That presentation described Iraq as a "tactical pivot" by which to transform the wider Middle East.

Brian Whitaker, former Guardian Middle East editor, rightly noted that the Perle-RAND strategy drew inspiration from a 1996 paper published by the Israeli Institute for Advanced Strategic and Political Studies, co-authored by Perle and other neocons who held top positions in the post-9/11 Bush administration.

The policy paper advocated a strategy that bears startling resemblance to the chaos unfolding in the wake of the expansion of the 'Islamic State' – Israel would "shape its strategic environment" by first securing the removal of Saddam Hussein. "Jordan and Turkey would form an axis along with Israel to weaken and 'roll back' Syria." This axis would attempt to weaken the influence of Lebanon, Syria and Iran by "weaning" off their Shi'ite populations. To succeed, Israel would need to engender US support, which would be obtained by Benjamin Netanyahu formulating the strategy "in language familiar to the Americans by tapping into themes of American administrations during the cold war."

The 2002 Perle-RAND plan was active in the Bush administration's strategic thinking on Iraq shortly before the 2003 war. According to US private intelligence firm Stratfor, in late 2002, then vice-president Dick Cheney and deputy defense secretary Paul Wolfowitz had co-authored a scheme under which central Sunni-majority Iraq would join with Jordan; the northern Kurdish regions would become an autonomous state; all becoming separate from the southern Shi'ite region.

The strategic advantages of an Iraq partition, Stratfor argued, focused on US control of oil: The expansion of the 'Islamic State' has provided a pretext for the fundamental contours of this scenario to unfold, with the US and British looking to re-establish a long-term military presence in Iraq in the name of the "defense of a young new state."

In 2006, Cheney's successor, Joe Biden, also indicated his support for the 'soft partition' of Iraq along ethno-religious lines – a position which the co-author of the Biden-Iraq plan, Leslie Gelb of the Council on Foreign Relations, now argues is "the only solution" to the current crisis.

Also in 2006, the Armed Forces Journal published a map of the Middle East with its borders thoroughly re-drawn, courtesy of Lt. Col. (ret.) Ralph Peters, who had previously been assigned to the Office of the Deputy Chief of Staff for Intelligence where he was responsible for future warfare. As for the goals of this plan, apart from "security from terrorism" and "the prospect of democracy", Peters also mentioned "access to oil supplies in a region that is destined to fight itself."

In 2008, the strategy re-surfaced – once again via RAND Corp – through a report funded by the US Army Training and Doctrine Command on how to prosecute the 'long war.' Among its strategies, one scenario advocated by the report was 'Divide and Rule' which would involve:

The Sionist strategy

Almost thirty years ago, a prominent group of neoconservative hawks found an effective vehicle for advocating their views via the Committee on the Present Danger, a group that fervently believed the United States was a hair away from being militarily surpassed by the Soviet Union, and whose raison d'être was strident advocacy of bigger military budgets, near-fanatical opposition to any form of arms control and zealous championing of a Likudnik Israel. Considered a marginal group in its nascent days during the Carter Administration, with the election of Ronald Reagan in 1980 CPD went from the margins to the center of power.

Just as the right-wing defense intellectuals made CPD a cornerstone of a shadow defense establishment during the Carter Administration, so, too, did the right during the Clinton years, in part through two organizations: the Jewish Institute for National Security Affairs (JINSA) and the Center for Security Policy (CSP). And just as was the case two decades ago, dozens of their members have ascended to powerful government posts, where their advocacy in support of the same agenda continues, abetted by the out-of-government adjuncts from which they came.

Industrious and persistent, they've managed to weave a number of issues--support for national missile defense, opposition to arms control treaties, championing of wasteful weapons systems, arms aid to Turkey and American unilateralism in general--into a hard line, with support for the Israeli right at its core.

On no issue is the JINSA/CSP hard line more evident than in its relentless campaign for war-- not just with Iraq, but "total war," as Michael Ledeen, one of the most influential JINSAns in Washington, put it last year. For this crew, "regime change" by any means necessary in Iraq, Iran, Syria, Saudi Arabia and the Palestinian Authority is an urgent imperative. Anyone who dissents--be it Colin Powell's State Department, the CIA or career military officers--is committing heresy against articles of faith that effectively hold there is no difference between US and Israeli national security interests, and that the only way to assure continued safety and prosperity for both countries is through hegemony in the Middle East--a hegemony achieved with the traditional cold war recipe of feints, force, clientism and covert action.

For example, the Pentagon's Defense Policy Board--chaired by JINSA/CSP adviser and former Reagan Administration Defense Department official Richard Perle, and stacked with advisers from both groups--recently made news by listening to a briefing that cast Saudi Arabia as an enemy to be brought to heel through a number of potential mechanisms, many of which mirror JINSA's recommendations, and which reflect the JINSA/CSP crowd's preoccupation with Egypt. (The final slide of the Defense Policy Board presentation proposed that "Grand Strategy for the Middle East" should concentrate on "Iraq as the tactical pivot, Saudi Arabia as the strategic pivot [and] Egypt as the prize.")

Ledeen has been leading the charge for regime change in Iran, while old comrades like Andrew Marshall and Harold Rhode in the Pentagon's Office of Net Assessment actively tinker with ways to re-engineer both the Iranian and Saudi governments. JINSA is also cheering the US military on as it tries to secure basing rights in the strategic Red Sea country of Eritrea, happily failing to mention that the once-promising secular regime of President Isaiais Afewerki continues to slide into the kind of repressive authoritarianism practiced by the "axis of evil" and its adjuncts.

Indeed, there are some in military and intelligence circles who have taken to using "axis of evil" in reference to JINSA and CSP, along with venerable repositories of hawkish thinking like the American Enterprise Institute and the Hudson Institute, as well as defense contractors, conservative foundations and public relations entities underwritten by far-right American Zionists (all of which help to underwrite JINSA and CSP).

It's a milieu where ideology and money seamlessly blend: "Whenever you see someone identified in print or on TV as being with the Center for Security Policy or JINSA championing a position on the grounds of ideology or principle--which they are unquestionably doing with conviction--you are, nonetheless, not informed that they're also providing a sort of cover for other ideologues who just happen to stand to profit from hewing to the Likudnik and Pax Americana lines," says a veteran intelligence officer.

JINSA / CSP

Founded in 1976 by neoconservatives concerned that the United States might not be able to provide Israel with adequate military supplies in the event of another Arab-Israeli war, over the past twenty-five years JINSA has gone from a loose-knit proto-group to a $1.4-million-a-year operation with a formidable array of Washington power players on its rolls.

Until the beginning of the previous Bush Administration, JINSA's board of advisers included such heavy hitters as Dick Cheney, John Bolton and Douglas Feith, the third-highest-ranking executive in the Pentagon during W. Bush administration. Both Perle and former Director of Central Intelligence James Woolsey, two of the loudest voices in the attack-Iraq chorus, are still on the board, as are such Reagan-era relics as Jeane Kirkpatrick, Eugene Rostow and Ledeen--Oliver North's Iran/*contra* liaison with the Israelis.

According to its website, JINSA exists to "educate the American public about the importance of an effective US defense capability so that our vital interests as Americans can be safeguarded" and to "inform the American defense and foreign affairs community about the important role Israel can and does play in bolstering democratic interests in the Mediterranean and the Middle East." In practice, this translates into its members producing a steady stream of op-eds and reports that have been good indicators of what the Pentagon's civilian leadership is thinking.

JINSA relishes denouncing virtually any type of contact between the US government and Syria and finding new ways to demonize the Palestinians. To give but one example (and one that kills two birds with one stone): According to JINSA, not only is Yasir Arafat in control of all violence in the occupied territories, but he orchestrates the violence solely "to protect Saddam.... Saddam is at the moment Arafat's only real financial supporter.... [Arafat] has no incentive to stop the violence against Israel and allow the West to turn its attention to his mentor and paymaster."

And if there's a way to advance other aspects of the far-right agenda by intertwining them with Israeli interests, JINSA doesn't hesitate there, either. A recent report contends that the Arctic National Wildlife Refuge must be tapped because "the Arab oil-producing states" are countries "with interests inimical to ours," but Israel "stand[s] with us when we need [Israel]," and a US policy of tapping oil under ANWR will "limit [the Arabs'] ability to do damage to either of us."

The bulk of JINSA's modest annual budget is spent on taking a bevy of retired US generals and admirals to Israel, where JINSA facilitates meetings between Israeli officials and the still-influential US flag officers, who, upon their return to the States, happily write op-eds and sign letters and advertisements championing the Likudnik line. (Sowing seeds for the future, JINSA also takes US service academy cadets to Israel each summer and sponsors a lecture series at the Army, Navy and Air Force academies.)

In one such statement, issued soon after the outbreak of the latest intifada, twenty-six JINSAns of retired flag rank, including many from the advisory board, struck a moralizing tone, characterizing Palestinian violence as a "perversion of military ethics" and holding that "America's role as facilitator in this process should never yield to America's responsibility as a friend to Israel," as "friends don't leave friends on the battlefield."

However high-minded this might sound, the post service associations of the letter's signatories--which are almost always left off the organization's website and communiqués--ought to require that the phrase be amended to say "friends don't leave friends on the battlefield, especially when there's business to be done and bucks to be made." Almost every retired officer who sits on JINSA's board of advisers or has participated in its Israel trips or signed a JINSA letter works or has worked with military contractors who do business with the Pentagon and Israel.

While some keep a low profile as self-employed "consultants" and avoid mention of their clients, others are less shy about their associations, including with the private mercenary firm Military Professional Resources International, weapons broker and military consultancy Cypress International and SY Technology, whose main clients include the Pentagon's Missile Defense Agency, which oversees several ongoing joint projects with Israel.

Military-Industrial Complex

The behemoths of military contracting are also well represented in JINSA's ranks. For example, JINSA advisory board members Adm. Leon Edney, Adm. David Jeremiah and Lieut. Gen. Charles May, all retired, have served Northrop Grumman or its subsidiaries as either consultants or board members. Northrop Grumman has built ships for the Israeli Navy and sold F-16 avionics and E-2C Hawkeye planes to the Israeli Air Force (as well as the Longbow radar system to the Israeli army for use in its attack helicopters).

It also works with Tamam, a subsidiary of Israeli Aircraft Industries, to produce an unmanned aerial vehicle. Lockheed Martin has sold more than $2 billion worth of F-16s to Israel since 1999, as well as flight simulators, multiple-launch rocket systems and Seahawk heavyweight torpedoes. At one time or another, General May, retired Lieut. Gen. Paul Cerjan and retired Adm. Carlisle Trost have labored in LockMart's vineyards. Trost has also sat on the board of General Dynamics, whose Gulfstream subsidiary has a $206 million contract to supply planes to Israel to be used for "special electronics missions."

By far the most profitably diversified of the JINSAns is retired Adm. David Jeremiah. President and partner of Technology Strategies & Alliances Corporation (described as a "strategic advisory firm and investment banking firm engaged primarily in the aerospace, defense, telecommunications and electronics industries"), Jeremiah also sits on the boards of Northrop Grumman's Litton subsidiary and of defense giant Alliant Techsystems, which--in partnership with Israel's TAAS--does a brisk business in rubber bullets. And he had a seat on the Pentagon's Defense Policy Board, chaired by Perle.

About the only major defense contractor without a presence on JINSA's advisory board is Boeing, which has had a relationship with Israeli Aircraft Industries for thirty years. (Boeing also sells F-15s to Israel and, in partnership with Lockheed Martin, Apache attack helicopters, a ubiquitous weapon in the occupied territories.)

But take a look at JINSA's kindred spirit in things pro-Likud and pro-Star Wars, the Center for Security Policy, and there on its national security advisory council are Stanley Ebner, a former Boeing executive; Andrew Ellis, vice president for government relations; and Carl Smith, a former staff director of the Senate Armed Services Committee who, as a lawyer in private practice, has counted Boeing among his clients. "JINSA and CSP," says a veteran Pentagon analyst, "may as well be one and the same."

Not a hard sell: There's always been considerable overlap beween the JINSA and CSP rosters--JINSA advisers Jeane Kirkpatrick, Richard Perle and Phyllis Kaminsky also served on CSP's advisory council; current JINSA advisory board chairman David Steinmann sits on CSP's board of directors; and before returning to the Pentagon Douglas Feith served as the board's chair. At this writing, twenty-two CSP advisers--including additional Reagan-era remnants like Elliott Abrams, Ken deGraffenreid, Paula Dobriansky, Sven Kraemer, Robert Joseph, Robert Andrews and J.D. Crouch--have reoccupied key positions in the national security establishment, as have other true believers of more recent vintage.

While CSP boasts an impressive advisory list of hawkish luminaries, its star is Frank Gaffney, its founder, president and CEO. A protégé of Perle going back to their days as staffers for the late Senator Henry "Scoop" Jackson (a k a the Senator from Boeing, and the Senate's most zealous champion of Israel in his day), Gaffney later joined Perle at the Pentagon, only to be shown the door by Defense Secretary Frank Carlucci in 1987, not long after Perle left.

Gaffney then reconstituted the latest incarnation of the Committee on the Present Danger. Beyond compiling an A-list of influential conservative hawks, Gaffney has been prolific over the past fifteen years, churning out a constant stream of reports (as well as regular columns for the *Washington Times*) making the case that the gravest threats to US national security are China, Iraq, still-undeveloped ballistic missiles launched by rogue states, and the passage of or adherence to virtually any form of arms control treaty.

Gaffney and CSP's prescriptions for national security have been fairly simple: Gut all arms control treaties, push ahead with weapons systems virtually everyone agrees should be killed (such as the V-22 Osprey), give no quarter to the Palestinians and, most important, go full steam ahead on just about every national missile defense program. (CSP was heavily represented on the late-1990s Commission to Assess the Ballistic Missile Threat to the United States, which was instrumental in keeping the program alive during the Clinton years.)

Looking at the center's affiliates, it's not hard to see why: Not only are makers of the Osprey (Boeing) well represented on the CSP's board of advisers but so too is Lockheed Martin (by vice president for space and strategic missiles Charles Kupperman and director of defense systems Douglas Graham). Former TRW executive Amoretta Hoeber is also a CSP adviser, as is former Congressman and Raytheon lobbyist Robert Livingston. Ball Aerospace & Technologies--a major manufacturer of NASA and Pentagon satellites--is represented by former Navy Secretary John Lehman, while missile-defense computer systems maker Hewlett-Packard is represented by George Keyworth, who is on its board of directors. And the Congressional Missile Defense Caucus and Osprey (or "tilt rotor") caucus are represented by Representative Curt Weldon and Senator Jon Kyl.

CSP was instrumental in developing the arguments against the Anti-Ballistic Missile Treaty. Largely ignored or derided at the time, a 1995 CSP memo co-written by Douglas Feith holding that the United States should withdraw from the ABM treaty has essentially become policy, as have other CSP reports opposing the Comprehensive Test Ban Treaty, the Chemical Weapons Convention and the International Criminal Court.

A Clean Break

But perhaps the most insightful window on the JINSA/CSP policy worldview comes in the form of a paper Perle and Feith collaborated on in 1996 with six others under the auspices of the Institute for Advanced Strategic and Political Studies. Essentially an advice letter to ascendant Israeli politician Benjamin Netanyahu, "A Clean Break: A New Strategy for Securing the Realm" makes for insightful reading as a kind of US-Israeli neoconservative manifesto.

The paper's first prescription was for an Israeli rightward economic shift, with tax cuts and a selloff of public lands and enterprises--moves that would also engender support from a "broad bipartisan spectrum of key pro-Israeli Congressional leaders." But beyond economics, the paper essentially reads like a blueprint for a mini-cold war in the Middle East, advocating the use of proxy armies for regime changes, destabilization and containment.

Indeed, it even goes so far as to articulate a way to advance right-wing Zionism by melding it with missile-defense advocacy. "Mr. Netanyahu can highlight his desire to cooperate more closely with the United States on anti-missile defense in order to remove the threat of blackmail which even a weak and distant army can pose to either state," it reads. "Not only would such cooperation on missile defense counter a tangible physical threat to Israel's survival, but it would broaden Israel's base of support among many in the United States Congress who may know little about Israel, but care very much about missile defense"-- something that has the added benefit of being "helpful in the effort to move the US embassy in Israel to Jerusalem."

Though the general agenda put forth by JINSA and CSP continues to be reflected in councils of war, even some of the hawks (including Rumsfeld deputy Paul Wolfowitz) are growing increasingly leery of Israel's settlements policy and Gaffney's relentless support for it. Indeed, his personal stock in Bush Administration circles is low. "Gaffney has worn out his welcome by being an overbearing gadfly rather than a serious contributor to policy," says a senior Pentagon political official. Since earlier this year, White House political adviser Karl Rove has been casting about for someone to start a new, more mainstream defense group that would counter the influence of CSP. According to those who have communicated with Rove on the matter, his quiet efforts are in response to complaints from many conservative activists who feel let down by Gaffney, or feel he's too hard on President Bush. "A lot of us have taken [Gaffney] at face value over the years," one influential conservative says. "Yet we now know he's pushed for some of the most flawed missile defense and conventional systems. He considered Cuba a 'classic asymmetric threat' but not Al Qaeda. And since 9/11, he's been less concerned with the threat to America than to Israel."

ISIS and Israel

Why is IS – formerly known as the Islamic State in Iraq and Syria (ISIS) – not fighting Israel? Would anything change if its fighters were to gain access to the borders with occupied Palestine?

While the Israeli military machine was massacring people in Gaza – and amid the euphoria among some jihadis over the news of the announcement of an "Islamic caliphate" – video footage of masked individuals firing rockets into Israel was posted online, and attributed to IS. Many cheered for what they saw as the "Muslim caliph's" response to calls for succor from the people of Gaza, even believing the "caliphate" was very close to liberating Jerusalem. But the euphoria did not last very long.

The video turned out to be from an old footage dating back to 2012, recorded by the militant group known as the Mujahideen Shura Council, and was repurposed to be attributed to IS. IS-affiliated social media activists such as Turujman al-Asawirti were also quick to question the authenticity of the video attributed to their group.

Al-Akhbar had a number of questions for IS supporters from Lebanon, Syria, and Iraq, including the following: Why has IS maintained its distance from the events in Palestine? Are the people of Gaza not Muslims after all? Does this posture not reinforce the premise that there is a hidden link between Zionism and Salafi-Jihadism that appeases Israel, or is geography alone to blame for their inaction?

In a speech by IS leader Abu Bakr al-Baghdadi, after he installed himself as caliph of the Muslims, he spoke about the terror inflicted on Palestine, but he did so only in passing, in the wider context of the terror Muslims face around the world.

In substance, they believe that liberating Palestine is irrelevant without the establishment of the caliphate in the countries surrounding Palestine first. Before him, in the time of the late leader of al-Qaeda Osama bin Laden, the jihadi attitude on Palestine was also controversial. Why have the jihadis never declared Palestine an arena for their jihad?

In effect, the leader of global jihadism Sheikh Ayman al-Zawahiri had an interesting position, approaching the issue from the angle of priorities on the basis of "Dar al-Kufr and Dar al-Islam," or the abode of disbelief and the abode of belief in jihadi lore. Zawahiri argues that fighting in Palestine should be on the basis that it is an abode of Islam, and that therefore, liberating it is a duty for every Muslim, as stated in his speech "truths about the conflict between Islam and infidelity" in 2007. But despite this, Palestine remains at the bottom of the list of priorities for most jihadis.

In form, most adherents of Salafi-Jihadism believe that "Shias are more dangerous than Jews." In substance, they believe that liberating Palestine is irrelevant without the establishment of the caliphate in the countries surrounding Palestine first.

Sources linked to IS told *Al-Akhbar*, "The final war that will liberate Palestine will be led by the caliphate, preceded by the establishment of this state in the Levant and Iraq," on the basis of sayings they attribute to Prophet Mohammad. The sources add, "Allah alone knows just how much the soldiers of the caliphate yearn for skipping the necessary stages and battle the Jews in Palestine, but he who rushes something before its time comes shall be punished by being denied it."

The sources, who are based in the Raqqa province of Syria, enumerate these necessary stages, saying, "The priority is to liberate Baghdad, then head to Damascus and liberate all of the Levant, before liberating Palestine."

This is the principle that IS soldiers follow: "Fighting nearby apostates is more important than fighting faraway infidels." To justify this, they rely on the Wars of Apostasy initiated by the Caliph Abu Bakr (against Muslims who renounced their religion following the death of the Prophet), who made it a priority over fighting infidels and Muslim conquests.

According to IS fighters, the adherents of all Islamic sects who do not submit to their "caliph" are either "apostates or misguided folk, who should be fought and killed, forced to repent and let themselves be guided, or be liberated from apostate rule." A jihadi adds here, "We the followers of this path follow sharia not the whims of men," adding that the Prophet had fought Quraysh first before moving on to fight the Jews of Banu Qurayza.

These sharia-based arguments are "reinforced" by the reality on the ground. A jihadi argues, "No one can initiate a battle against Israel except through the [direct] borders." The jihadi then adds sarcastically, "Certainly, the mujahideen will not be able to bomb Israel by air," before he said, "IS is still far from Israel. If it reaches Jordan and southern Syria (the Golan and Quneitra), then things would be different."

The jihadis base their vision on their perception that "Syria, Lebanon, Egypt, and Jordan all collaborate with Israel," and argue that any attack they initiate would be stopped by what they call the "idolatry" regimes in the name of security. A jihadi opines, "Since the countries adjacent to Israel do not fire a single bullet at it, this means they do not want a confrontation with Israel. Any attempt to use their territories to target Israel means automatically a confrontation with these regimes. Therefore, we must first purge these countries to get to Israel."

The IS-affiliated jihadis conclude that "the enmity the Arab countries and Arab groups have with Israel are in words not deeds, that is, only in politics and slogans. As long as this is the case, any group that wants to operate will confront these regimes." As proof of their point, the jihadis give the example of the Abdullah Azzam Brigades' operations out of South Lebanon, and the subsequent crackdown on the group's members after they fired rockets into Israel. For this reason, these jihadis believe that the priority is for their "state" to expand gradually, and that everything else is meaningless and illogical.

With regards to suicide operations, the jihadis said, "This is on the table, but the time for it has not yet come."

Mossad's chiefs about Iran

Meir Dagan

Former Mossad Chief Meir Dagan said that he would have resigned if Prime Minister Benjamin Netanyahu had decided to attack Iran's nuclear facilities. In his interview with Channel 10, Dagan said, "it was his fully within his authority to make such a decision, but I decided that I would resign at that moment."

In the interview, Dagan also showed the letter in which he requested to leave his post – responding to claims made by Netanyahu's associates that his criticism of the premier was due to personal reasons, after Netanyahu decided not to renew his tenure. "It hurts me that the prime minister is not telling the truth. This is simply not true. I can show you a letter I wrote to the prime minister, that I sent him, and I asked to end my term."

Dagan has granted several interviews over the last few weeks, criticizing Netanyahu's policies and behaviors, and headlined a left-wing rally in Tel Aviv, in which he said that Israel faces its worst crisis ever under Netanyahu's leadership.

Likud officials said of Dagan's speech that it was "strange that he now claims that he doesn't have faith in the current leadership, when he himself requested to extend his tenure as Mossad chief under the leadership of the prime minister.

In his resignation letter, presented on Channel 10, Dagan wrote: "*Sir, as you know, I conclude my tenure on 1/1/11. I recommend that a candidate be chosen in the near future to take on the task of Mossad chief, so that we can properly prepare him and ensure that his entrance into the position be as smooth as possible. If you would like to consult with me about a candidate, I am happy to do so. As such, I am concluding 42 years in the service of the state. I did the best that I could. I want to thank you for the faith and support that I received from you, and to thank Mr. Ariel Sharon who appointed me to the position, and Mr. Ehud Olmert, under whom I worked. I would also like to take this opportunity to wish you and your family and all of Israel and good and blessed year. Respectfully, Meir Dagan*."

During the interview with Channel 10, Dagan also expressed his support for Labor chief Isaac Herzog as prime minister: "In my eyes, he is not just a fitting candidate, but at this time, he seems to me to be the very best candidate to take on the role of prime minister."

Tamir Prado

Tamir Pardo, head of Mossad, had this to say to a roomful of Israeli ambassadors:

"What is the significance of the term existential threat?" the ambassadors quoted Pardo as asking. "Does Iran pose a threat to Israel? Absolutely. But if one said a nuclear bomb in

Iranian hands was an existential threat, that would mean that we would have to close up shop and go home. That's not the situation. The term existential threat is used too freely."

Not only is Pardo going on the record to say that this language, favored by the very Prime Minister who appointed him to head Mossad, is overblown, but he did it in front of a roomful of Avigdor Lieberman's people. This takes guts: Defense Minister Ehud Barak recently found himself in trouble for going off message on Iran when he suggested that Israel is not the sole motive force behind Iran's nuclear talk.

Officially, Israel continues to criticize the talks and the pending nuclear agreement between the world powers and Iran. Prime Minister Benjamin Netanyahu and Defense Minister Moshe Ya'alon, each in his own way, keep bashing the negotiations.

It will take nearly three more months to flesh out the full details of a final and comprehensive agreement. President Obama says Iran's nuclear program will be reduced and rolled back so that it would take one year to "break out" to assemble a bomb. In return the West and the UN's sanctions will be gradually lifted.

Most Israeli experts, and certainly its leaders, have argued without hesitation that the current deal is dangerous to Israel's interests. But is it really? The blatant reality is that even before the deal Iran was already a nuclear threshold state. And if it really wants to, it can run off and produce nuclear weapons.

On the other hand, Israel is the strongest nation in the region. According to foreign reports, the only democracy in the Middle East boasts both a significant nuclear arsenal and submarines that are capable of executing second strikes — the capability to respond to a nuclear attack with powerful nuclear retaliation.

Four Arab states — Syria, Iraq, Libya and Yemen — are disintegrating. As a result, Israel's strategic posture has improved, as many of the serious military threats facing Israel have dissipated.

Israel would have preferred that there be no negotiations on Iran's nuclear ambitions, and that sanctions would be in place forever. But that won't happen. Without admitting it, Israel is preparing itself for the "day after," adjusting its position to the reality at the end of the negotiations.

The world will never hear an official admission, but deep in their heart Israeli leaders surely understand they failed to orchestrate an international campaign against the talks and the deal that has emerged.
It was an unnecessary campaign. Israel paid a heavy price in its confrontation with the US administration, and it caused great animosity between Netanyahu and President Barack Obama. Frankly, Israel had very little influence, if at all, on the talks.

The only tangible result was that Netanyahu won reelection last month, after convincing the public that only he knows how to deal with the threat of Iran becoming a nuclear state.

But now, with election season over and the deal with Iran being shaped, Israel has started clandestine diplomatic and intelligence initiatives to reach understandings and define red lines on how to deal with the upcoming reality.

Israeli bodies – the Defense Ministry, the air force, Military Intelligence and the Mossad – are already involved in discreet contacts with their American counterparts, as well as with EU countries, on how to prepare various responses in case Iran violates the deal.

The best-case scenario is that Iran will adhere to the agreement. But anyone who follows Iran's nuclear history and its relations with international bodies such as the International Atomic Energy Agency knows that it is unlikely to happen. Most probably Iran will try to dishonor its obligations through deceptions and lies.

Israel, with its counterparts, is trying to define the possible responses needed if and when Iran's deceptions are exposed. In the past, international media reported that Mossad chiefs met with their Saudi counterparts to coordinate joint efforts to stop Iran from building nuclear bombs. In these reports it said Saudi Arabia agreed that the Israel Air Force would use Saudi airspace for an attack on Iran's nuclear sites.

This doesn't mean that Israel is already coordinating a detailed military option with all those who are against the deal. These exchanges are more about reaching a basic understanding, should Iran seriously violate the deal.

Indeed, one should not hastily reach the conclusion that Israel is expediting its preparations to strike Iran. For now, Israel is still relying on the Americans. Ya'alon made it clear that Obama had promised that he would not allow Iran to have nuclear weapons.

But it is also clear that Israel will not tolerate a situation where Iran is on the verge of producing nuclear bombs. In such a worst-case scenario, it is most probable that any Israeli prime minister will make the same decision as previous leaders – Menachem Begin in 1981 and Ehud Olmert in 2007, who ordered to destroy Iraqi and Syrian nuclear reactors, respectively. Even though it's reported that Israel does have nuclear weapons it can't allow Iran, which advocates the destruction of the Jewish state, to have nuclear bombs.